U.S. ARMED FORCES

The U.S. Air Force

Sandy Donovan

LERNER PUBLICATIONS COMPANY / MINNEAPOLIS

CHAPTER OPENER PHOTO CAPTIONS

Cover: The view from the cockpit of a Thunderbird F-16 as the team flies in close formation. The Thunderbirds, the air force's performance flying team, performs its daring act at air shows around the United States.

Ch. 1: U.S. Army Air Service Spad S. XIII aircraft take off from an airstrip in France during World War I (1914–1918). U.S. pilots fought German fliers over the trenches and battlefields of Europe during this war.

Ch. 2: All air force recruits must take an oath to defend the United States.

Ch. 3: Cadets march in formation during a day of training at the U.S. Air Force Academy. Training teaches cadets to be part of a team while leading others. The common goal of all airmen is to defend the United States.

Ch. 4: Two F-16 Fighting Falcon pilots return from a mission. U.S. Air Force pilots are among the best trained in the world, and they fly some of the most advanced aircraft ever built.

Copyright © 2005 by Sandy Donovan

Lerner Publications Company
A division of Lerner Publishing Group
241 First Avenue North
Minneapolis, MN 55401 U.S.A.

Website address: www.lernerbooks.com

Library of Congress Cataloging-in-Publication Data

Donovan, Sandra, 1967–
    The U.S. Air Force / by Sandy Donovan
        p.   cm. — (U.S. Armed Forces)
    Includes biographical references and index.
        Contents: History — Recruitment — Training — Life in the Air Force.
        ISBN: 0-8225-1436-2 (lib. bdg. : alk. paper)
        1. United States. Air Force—Juvenile literature. [1. United States. Air Force.] I. Title.
    II. Series: U.S. Armed Forces (Series : Lerner Publications)
    UG633.D62 2005
    358.4'00973—dc22   2003019048

Manufactured in the United States of America
1 2 3 4 5 6 — JR — 10 09 08 07 06 05

CONTENTS

chapter ONE

HISTORY

THE U.S. ARMED FORCES have
four major branches—the army, navy, Marine Corps,
and air force. The air force is the youngest branch. It
was created in 1947. But the U.S. military has used
aircraft since the early 1900s.

In 1903 Orville and Wilbur Wright made the world's
first airplane flight in North Carolina. Soon the U.S.
Army was interested in airplanes. Army leaders
thought airplanes would be useful in war. In 1907 they
created the U.S. Army Air Service (AAS).

WORLD WARS

The AAS trained pilots and bought aircraft.
Meanwhile, in Europe, World War I had started.
Many armies were already flying planes in combat,
or battle.

In 1917 the United States joined this war. They
joined the Allies—Russia, Britain, France, and others.
The Allies fought against the Central powers of
Germany, Austria-Hungary, and others. Both sides
flew airplanes called biplanes, which have two sets of
wings. At first, these aircraft were used only for
reconnaissance—to fly over the enemy and gather
information.

After a while,
enemy planes began to
clash. They fought in
dogfights. In a
dogfight, enemy
aircraft shoot at each
other. They try to
knock each other out
of the sky. In 1918 the
Central powers
surrendered. With the
help of the U.S. Army
Air Service, the Allies
had won the war.

Twenty-one years
later, World War II
(1939–1945) began in
Europe. The United

Biplanes fought for control of
the skies during World War I.
Dogfights often involved
dozens of aircraft.

States joined the Allies in 1941. They fought against the Axis powers of Germany, Japan, Italy, and other nations. During World War II, the AAS changed its name to the army air forces (AAF).

Aircraft technology had grown since the last war. Airplanes were faster, more powerful, and could fly much farther than before. They played a major role in the fighting. AAF airplanes flew reconnaissance missions deep into enemy territory. Waves of long-range bombers dropped bombs on German factories and cities. After years of bombing, the Germans found it hard to build effective weapons.

AAF fighter planes flew along on the bombing missions. The fast, agile fighters protected the large, slow bombers from enemy attack planes.

AAF fighters and bombers also supported

JACQUELINE COCHRAN, PIONEER PILOT

Jacqueline "Jackie" Cochran *(above)* was the leader of the Women's Airforce Service Pilots (WASPs), a unit of women pilots created during World War II. At that time, women were not allowed to fly in combat. So WASP pilots performed noncombat flight duties, freeing up male pilots to fight. WASPs ferried, or delivered, aircraft from factories to military bases around the world. From 1942 to 1944, WASPs flew about 60 million miles, delivering more than 12,000 planes for the war effort.

Cochran was one of the finest aviators of her time. A mostly self-trained pilot, she began flying in air races in the 1930s, winning many trophies. In the 1950s, she became the first woman to fly faster than the speed of sound. In 1964 she set a new world record, reaching 1,429 miles per hour.

Near the end of World War II, an AAF bomber dropped an atomic bomb on the Japanese city of Hiroshima *(above)*. The city was leveled, and the powerful new superweapon convinced the Japanese to surrender.

Allied troops on the ground. Swooping low over the battlefield, the planes destroyed enemy targets. These attacks helped clear the way for Allied armies. In May 1945, Germany surrendered. World War II in Europe was over.

Meanwhile, in Asia and the Pacific, AAF bombers and fighters attacked Japanese targets. In early August 1945, AAF bombers dropped atomic bombs on two Japanese cities, Hiroshima and Nagasaki. These powerful weapons destroyed the cities and killed tens of thousands of Japanese. A few days later, Japan surrendered. World War II was over.

A SEPARATE AIR FORCE

World War II proved that aircraft were important in battle. In 1947 U.S. leaders decided the air force should be a separate part of the U.S. military. The U.S. Air Force (USAF) was created.

Aircraft technology continued to improve. A new kind of aircraft engine, called the jet engine, was developed. Jet power helped planes to fly up to 600 miles per hour. A way to refuel airplanes in the air was also invented. This meant that bombers and other military planes could fly all over the world without having to land and refuel.

STRATEGIC AIR COMMAND

After World War II, the United States and the Soviet Union became enemies. This period became known as

BRIGADIER GENERAL CHARLES E. YEAGER

Charles E. "Chuck" Yeager (above) was a successful World War II fighter pilot. He later became one of the air force's best test pilots. During the war, Yeager saw action in Europe, where he shot down 13 German aircraft. He himself was once shot down over enemy territory. But he avoided capture and flew again. On October 12, 1944, he shot down five enemy aircraft.

Following the war, Yeager became a test pilot, working on a program that tested rocket-driven aircraft. On October 14, 1947, flying the X-1S rocket plane, he became the first person to achieve supersonic flight (flying faster than the speed of sound). In the following years, Yeager continued to test the air force's newest aircraft. He retired in 1975.

the Cold War (1945–1991). The two countries did not fight one another, but they remained enemies.

In 1949 the Soviet Union developed its own atomic bomb. From that time, both countries feared the other might try to attack first. The air force had the job of defending the United States from air attack. To do this, the USAF created the Strategic Air Command (SAC). If war broke out, SAC was also responsible for attacking the Soviet Union.

SAC had at least a dozen nuclear-armed bombers in the air at all times. The bombers circled near the Soviet Union, ready to attack at a moment's notice. U.S. leaders believed this deterred (discouraged) the Soviet Union from striking the United States first.

THE KOREAN WAR

The Korean War (1950–1953) started when North Korea invaded South Korea. The United States and many other nations supported South Korea. China and the Soviet Union supported North Korea.

Jet fighter planes fought for control of the skies over Korea. The USAF used a powerful new plane called the F-86 Sabre. F-86 pilots shot down almost 800 enemy planes during the war. Fewer than 60 Sabres were shot down.

After the Korean War ended, the United States and the Soviet Union remained enemies. The two countries developed new technology for nuclear war. Each side built rocket-powered intercontinental ballistic missiles (ICBMs). ICBMs could travel thousands of miles—from one continent to another—to make nuclear attacks.

During the Korean War, USAF F-86 Sabres *(above)* battled North Korean and Chinese pilots in the skies over Korea.

SAC was responsible for the United States' ICBMs. A huge SAC headquarters was built at Offutt Air Force Base, near Omaha, Nebraska. From there, SAC used radar (a system that detects objects in the air), computers, and other equipment to track the skies of North America. SAC systems were always on the watch for Soviet invaders.

Rockets also sent people and equipment into space. By the late 1950s, the United States and the Soviet Union were developing spacecraft. Many of the first U.S. astronauts were air force officers.

By the 1960s, the USAF had developed a system of satellites that circled the earth. These satellites took pictures and gathered information about the Soviet Union and other countries. They also gathered information about weather around the world.

VIETNAM WAR

In the late 1950s, North Vietnam and South Vietnam were fighting one another to control the entire country. The United States fought on the side of the South Vietnamese. By the mid-1960s, thousands of U.S. soldiers were fighting in the Vietnam War. Meanwhile, China and the Soviet Union were giving the North Vietnamese weapons and equipment.

The U.S. Air Force played a major role in the Vietnam War. USAF fighter planes—such as the F-4 Phantom—attacked enemy targets on the ground.

The supersonic F-4 Phantom carries many different kinds of bombs and missiles.

They also fought North Vietnamese aircraft in the skies over Vietnam. The F-4 is fast and powerful. It can fly up to 1,500 miles per hour.

The B-52 Stratofortress is a high-altitude heavy bomber.

Huge USAF B-52 bombers flew high above North Vietnam. From there they dropped thousands of tons of bombs on North Vietnamese factories and other targets.

U.S. forces defeated the North Vietnamese in every major battle. But the North Vietnamese refused to give up. After many years of fighting, U.S. forces pulled out of Vietnam in the early 1970s. By 1975 the North Vietnamese had defeated the South Vietnamese. Vietnam became a single nation.

THE COLD WAR ENDS

In the early 1990s, the Soviet Union peacefully split into several separate countries. The Cold War was over. With the Soviet threat gone, SAC was no longer needed. It was shut down.

To respond to new world threats, the United States continued building new and better aircraft and missiles. These included the F-15 Eagle and the F-16 Fighting Falcon.

A new kind of
weapon, called the
cruise missile, was
also developed. Cruise
missiles can travel
thousands of miles to
strike their targets.
They fly so low and fast
that they are difficult to
detect and shoot down.
And air force pilots
continued to pilot
spacecraft, such as the
space shuttle.

In 1990 the Middle
Eastern country of Iraq
invaded its neighbor
Kuwait. The U.S.
government formed a
coalition, or group, of
many countries to
remove Iraqi forces
from Kuwait. Iraqi

F-15 Eagles can fly at more than
twice the speed of sound.

president Saddam Hussein refused to leave Kuwait, so
coalition forces attacked. This led to the Persian Gulf
War (1991).

USAF pilots and aircraft played a major role in the
war. Air force pilots bombed Iraqi military targets. A new
kind of fighter, the F-117 Nighthawk, bombed targets in
Baghdad, the Iraqi capital. Air force planes also flew
army troops and supplies to where they were needed.

The F-117 Nighthawk uses stealth technology to make it almost invisible to radar. Part of that technology is the plane's unusual shape. Flying at night, the Nighthawk can fly in and out of enemy territory undetected.

Coalition forces, led by the United States, overwhelmed the Iraqi army. Saddam Hussein's forces were pushed out of Kuwait in just a few weeks.

After the war, Hussein's forces attacked the Kurds—a group of people living in northern Iraq. To protect the Kurds from Iraqi attacks, USAF and British Royal Air Force (RAF) pilots created a "no-fly zone" over northern Iraq. Iraqi aircraft were not allowed to fly in this zone. USAF and RAF pilots patrolled the no-fly zone throughout the 1990s.

The air force also assisted and protected people in other parts of the world. In 1992 U.S. troops went to the African country of Somalia to help millions of

WOMEN IN THE AIR FORCE

For many years, women were not allowed to become air force pilots. This is because women were not allowed to serve in combat. But in 1993, this rule was changed, and since then, women have become some of the best air force pilots.

Lieutenant Colonel Stayce D. Harris *(above)* is the first African American woman to lead a USAF flying squadron. She serves in the U.S. Air Force Reserves as vice commander of the 507th Air Refueling Wing. This unit flies fuel tankers that can refuel other aircraft while in flight. Harris is also a pilot for United Airlines.

starving people there. Air force pilots flew in food and other supplies.

In the 1990s, the United States also became involved in a bloody war in eastern Europe. The citizens of Serbia, Croatia, Bosnia-Herzegovina, and Slovenia were fighting each other. The United Nations, a worldwide peacekeeping group, sent troops to the area to keep peace. The U.S. Air Force helped the United Nations troops. Air force pilots patrolled the skies and prevented other countries from fighting in the area.

In 1999 the United States and other European countries stepped in to protect people in a region of Serbia known as Kosovo. Thousands of Kosovars were being murdered by Serbian forces. USAF planes attacked Serbian targets. The USAF used a new kind of bomber during these battles—the B-2 Spirit.

Like the F-117, the B-2 uses stealth technology. In Kosovo, it soared through enemy territory undetected, hitting targets with pinpoint accuracy.

WAR IN AFGHANISTAN

On September 11, 2001, terrorists attacked the United States. They hijacked airplanes and flew them into buildings. The terrorists destroyed the World Trade Center towers in New York City and damaged the Pentagon, the U.S. military headquarters near Washington, D.C. About 3,000 people were killed.

Within 24 hours, air force personnel were at the disaster scenes, helping with rescue efforts. Air force

Air force airmen prepare an F-15 Eagle for a mission to Afghanistan in 2001.

doctors treated many wounded people. Meanwhile, USAF fighters patrolled the skies over the United States, ready to stop another terrorist attack.

The U.S. government believes that a terrorist group called al-Qaeda was responsible for the attacks. The U.S. government knew that the leaders of Afghanistan helped al-Qaeda. These leaders were called the Taliban. The Taliban gave al-Qaeda money and allowed it to train in Afghanistan.

After the September 11 attacks, U.S. president George W. Bush asked the Taliban to hand over the al-Qaeda terrorists in Afghanistan. The Taliban refused. In October 2001, the United States attacked the Taliban and the al-Qaeda terrorist camps. B-2s and B-52s bombed al-Qaeda and Taliban bases. F-15s and F-16s also destroyed enemy targets.

U.S. forces used other modern weapons to fight the war. New bombs, called "smart bombs," were extremely accurate. They could be dropped from thousands of feet in the air and hit targets within inches of their mark.

After only a few months, the al-Qaeda camps were destroyed. Taliban forces were crushed. A new Afghan government was set up.

THE SECOND GULF WAR

In 2002 leaders in the U.S. government were worried that Saddam Hussein was trying to build nuclear bombs and other dangerous weapons. The United Nations ordered him to give up his dangerous weapons. The Iraqi president claimed that he had no such weapons.

The United States formed another coalition to force Saddam Hussein out of power.

On March 17, 2003, President Bush ordered Saddam Hussein to leave Iraq. When Saddam refused, coalition forces invaded the country. USAF aircraft and personnel once again played a key role in the war. Aircraft dropped smart bombs on thousands of targets in Iraq. USAF planes provided close air support (CAS) to coalition troops on the ground. On CAS missions, ground troops spotted Iraqi targets and called in aircraft. The aircraft destroyed the targets, clearing the way for the troops.

The coalition forces quickly destroyed Saddam Hussein's army. Within three weeks, U.S. forces

Airmen prepare a B-1 Lancer for combat in Iraq. The air force has a fleet of 60 of these supersonic heavy bombers.

An air force helicopter drops airmen in Iraq in 2003.

were rolling through Baghdad. Saddam Hussein's government was destroyed.

After major combat had ended, many USAF units left Iraq. Some of these returned home to train for future missions, wherever they may be. Some units stayed in Iraq to help with the rebuilding of the country and to patrol the skies against threats to coalition forces.

chapter TWO

RECRUITMENT

MOST U.S. CITIZENS over the age of
17 are able to enlist in, or join, the air force. Most
members of the air force team are enlisted personnel.
They perform many different duties. Officers are the
leaders of the air force. They receive more schooling
and training.

Recruits can enter service full-time or part-time.
More than 350,000 people serve full-time on active
duty in the air force. About 250,000 serve part-time in
the U.S. Air Force Reserve.

AIRMEN: ENLISTED PERSONNEL

Airmen, or enlisted air force members, usually have support jobs, such as repairing aircraft and handling weapons. A U.S. citizen can enlist in the air force right after high school. Most high schools have counselors or recruiters to help people decide if enlistment is the right decision for them. A person who wants to enlist is called a candidate.

Candidates must meet certain requirements to join the air force. They must be high school graduates, and they must be between the ages of 17 and 28.

Before enlistment, a recruiter *(right)* will discuss the many different career options with an air force candidate.

Candidates who are 17 must have their parents' permission to enlist.

The first step for candidates is an exam called the Armed Services Vocational Aptitude Battery (ASVAB). This test looks at language, math, science, and problem-solving skills. The results of the test are used to figure out what type of air force job would be best for that person.

Once candidates pass the ASVAB test, they are sent to a military entrance processing station. These offices are located in cities across the United States. At the processing stations, candidates have to prove that they are U.S. citizens or plan to soon become U.S. citizens. Doctors also check each candidate for general health. Once candidates pass the physical exam, they set up an appointment with an air force counselor.

The counselor's job is to match candidates' interests with the jobs available in the air force. The counselor looks at the ASVAB results to help figure out the best air force career choice. Finally, the candidate signs a contract to make a four-year commitment to be a full-time member of the U.S. Air Force. Reservists commit to eight years of service when they sign up.

OFFICER CANDIDATES: AIR FORCE ACADEMY

A second way to enter the air force is to train to be an officer. To be an air force pilot, you must be an officer.

Just like enlisted personnel, officer candidates must meet certain requirements. All new officers must be between the ages of 18 and 30. They must also be college graduates. But candidates can train to become officers while they are in college. For these people, the air force offers several officer training programs. Candidates enter the two largest of these programs when they start college. They are the Air Force Academy (AFA) in Colorado Springs, Colorado,

Air Force Academy instructors constantly challenge cadets (military students). They push cadets to be the best they can be.

and the Reserve Officer Training Corps (ROTC). The corps has locations in many colleges throughout the United States. Both of these programs help officer candidates pay for college. In return, the students pledge to do four to ten years of air force duty once they graduate.

The AFA trains some of the brightest young people in the country to become air force officers. Most AFA graduates become pilots. But getting accepted into the AFA is quite difficult. Only about one in 100 candidates are admitted.

Many people begin preparing for the AFA while they are freshmen in high school. To get accepted, students need to do well in math, science, and language courses. They also need high scores on standardized tests such as the Scholastic Aptitude Test, or SAT.

EARNING A COLLEGE DEGREE

Recruits can earn college degrees while in the air force. They can take free college courses through the air force's correspondence (mail) school. The air force also helps with tuition costs if an airman wants to take classes at a college near an airman's base. And recruits can earn college credits without even going to a single class. In the Community College of the Air Force (CCAF), the air force keeps track of all the training a recruit goes through and converts it into college credits. These credits can sometimes turn out to equal a full degree.

This is a test taken by most college-bound high school students. The SAT grades a student's knowledge in subjects such as math, reading, and science. Students also need to participate in activities and athletics.

Candidates start applying to the AFA during their junior year of high school. They complete a questionnaire with a local AFA admissions officer. Most high school guidance counselors have information on whom to contact.

AFA candidates must be between 17 and 23 years old. They cannot be married or have children.

ROTC cadets gain valuable experience and a good education. About 60 percent of air force officers received their training in the ROTC.

Candidates often need a recommendation from their U.S. senator or representative to go along with their application. They also have to pass more tests, including a medical exam. Candidates find out if they are accepted to the AFA during their senior year of high school.

ROTC programs are located on 144 college and university campuses nationwide.

OFFICER CANDIDATES: RESERVE OFFICER TRAINING CORPS (ROTC) AND OFFICER TRAINING SCHOOL (OTS)

Most candidates become officers through the ROTC program. ROTC units are located at colleges and universities across the country. Air Force ROTC students study how to be an air force officer while they are in college. ROTC is a four-year program that helps students pay for college and trains them to be military leaders.

Students apply for the Air Force ROTC program when they apply for college. The first step in doing this is talking to a local ROTC recruiter. Recruiters are located in recruiting offices throughout the United States. The recruiter explains the ROTC process to the candidate and answers any questions. The recruiter also helps a candidate apply for the program. To be accepted, a candidate has to pass a written test and a physical exam.

College graduates can also train to become air force officers. The air force has a special program for college graduates called Officer Training School (OTS). OTS is a 12-week school that prepares men and women to be officers.

AIR FORCE SONG:
Off we go into the wild blue yonder,
Climbing high into the sun;
Here they come zooming to meet our thunder.
At 'em boys, Give 'er the gun!
    (Give 'er the gun now!)
Down we dive, spouting our flame from under,
Off with one heck of a roar!
We live in fame or go down in flame. Hey!
Nothing'll stop the U.S. Air Force!

UNIFORMS

ALL ON-DUTY PERSONNEL are expected to be in
uniform. Members' names, ranks, and jobs can
all be learned by a quick glance at their
uniforms. Air force personnel have different
uniforms for different occasions, jobs, and
roles. These include dress uniforms,
flight suits, and battle dress uniforms.

SERVICE, OR "DRESS BLUE," UNIFORM

Dress blues are most often
worn on ceremonial occasions,
during parades for example,
or formal military events.

"BLUES"

Blues are a simpler version of the
dress blue uniform. Air force personnel
often wear blues for everyday duties.

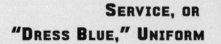

FLIGHT SUIT

Flight suits are worn by pilots and air crews. Fighter pilots wear special suits called G-suits (gravity suits). The suits help to keep the pilot from "graying out" due to loss of blood to the head during high-speed combat. The G-suits help limit the flow of blood to a pilot's arms and legs when a plane makes "high g-force" moves, such as tight turns, rolls, climbs, and dives.

BATTLE DRESS UNIFORM

Battle dress uniforms, or BDUs, are worn in the field (in combat conditions), as well as on air bases. This BDU has a forest camouflage pattern. Its colors and patterns are designed to blend in with the forest. This makes wearers harder to see— and safer—during combat.

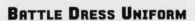

To enter OTS, candidates must take the Air Force Officer Qualification Test (AFOQT). The AFOQT is a series of tests that measure how well a candidate might do in a variety of jobs. For instance, some of the tests look specifically for the skills needed to be a pilot.

During the 12 weeks of OTS, officer candidates go through military, academic, and physical training. Before graduation, they are tested in all these areas. They must pass written tests as well as physical tests. Once the candidates pass these tests, they are ready to serve in the U.S. Air Force.

chapter THREE

TRAINING

ONCE A PERSON is accepted into an air force training program, the real work begins. Whether joining as an enlisted member or training to be an officer, air force training is difficult.

BASIC TRAINING

After enlisting in the air force, a candidate is called a recruit. All recruits go through basic military training at Lackland Air Force Base near San Antonio, Texas. Basic training is usually called boot camp.

When the new recruits arrive, they are often called the "rainbow" crew. This is because they are all wearing different colors of clothes. Once boot camp begins, they will all be wearing the same color— military green.

The first stop for new recruits is the barber's chair. Men have all their hair shaved off. Women have their hair cut short. When the barber is done, the recruits have the same look. This is the beginning of a process.

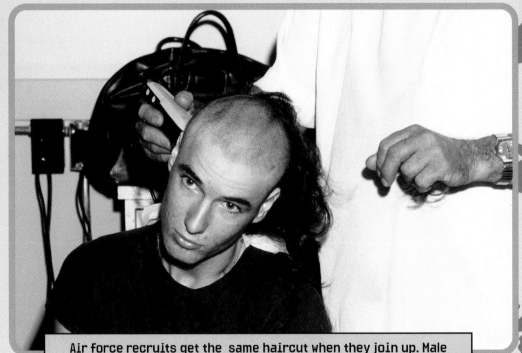

Air force recruits get the same haircut when they join up. Male recruits have their heads shaved. Women have their hair cut short.

During boot camp, recruits will learn to think of themselves as one part of a team.

After the barber's chair, new recruits are assigned to a flight. A flight is a class of about 30 to 60 people.

This group of recruits will stay together through all of basic training. They will take classes together, exercise together, and sleep in the same dorm. Air force basic training lasts six weeks.

Boot camp days are filled from sunup to sundown. Recruits wake up at 5:00 A.M. Exercise time, called physical conditioning, is first on the schedule. Next come showers, breakfast, and dorm room inspections. Recruits are expected to keep their bunks and lockers perfectly clean and organized.

Recruits spend the rest of their morning in classes. At lunch they all eat together and then return to classes. Afternoon classes are followed by military training and another inspection. Then come dinner and study time before lights out at 9:00 P.M.

A boot camp drill sergeant *(standing)* takes recruits through their morning physical conditioning.

The final week of boot camp is called Warrior Week. During Warrior Week, all recruits live in tents at a special camp. The instructors act as the enemy and attack the camp to teach and test the recruits' combat skills. The recruits must learn how to defend the camp to complete their training.

During Warrior Week, instructors *(above)* push recruits *(below)* to their limits. If they can pass the test, recruits will become air force airmen.

After Warrior Week, recruits are officially called airmen. All enlisted members of the air force are called airmen, even if they are women. Airmen have a graduation ceremony on the last day of camp. Then they are ready for active duty.

All enlisted members of the air force are called airmen, even if they are women.

AIR FORCE ACADEMY

At the Air Force Academy, new students are called cadets. When cadets arrive, they are assigned to a dorm room with a roommate. The air force pays for their classes and meals and gives them a monthly allowance.

Cadets begin their first year at the academy with basic cadet training. This training is a lot like boot camp. It includes exercise, military drills, and a field training camp. Once they finish this training, cadets become a member of the cadet wing, or the student body.

For their first two years at the academy, cadets take many of the same classes as students at other colleges. They study math, language, science, and other subjects. Cadets also take many classes on military tactics, or ways to fight.

After their first two years, cadets choose a special area of study. Most cadets take flying lessons. They will learn to fly the newest air force planes.

Tools of the Trade

THE AIR FORCE HAS A LARGE FLEET OF AIRCRAFT.

Each type is designed to perform an important role. Some aircraft are used for combat. Others work in support tasks.

BOMBERS

The B-2 Spirit bomber uses stealth technology. It can fly in and out of enemy territory without being detected on radar. The B-2's specialty is hitting important targets in a moment's notice.

FIGHTERS

The F-16 Fighting Falcon is a fast and maneuverable fighter. It can be used to fight other aircraft or to attack targets on the ground.

TANKER AIRCRAFT

The KC-10A Extender is the air force's newest airborne refueling tanker. Tanker aircraft use a long tube, called a boom, to refuel aircraft while in flight. Airborne refueling allows aircraft to fly long missions, such as extended combat missions or flights from one continent to another.

Transport Aircraft

The C-17 Globemaster is the air force's newest cargo plane. It can carry up to 102 troops or paratroopers or 170,900 pounds of equipment. Airborne refueling allows the C-17 to fly around the world without stopping.

Command, Control, and Communications Aircraft

The E-3 Sentry is an airborne warning and control system (AWACS) aircraft. Flying high over the battlefield, the E-3 works as a combat air traffic controller. Its radar system (the rotating disc on top of the plane) detects, identifies, and tracks both enemy and friendly aircraft within a 250-mile range.

Attack Aircraft

The A-10 Thunderbolt II, or "Warthog," is an attack aircraft, designed to hit ground targets, such as tanks and buildings. It is heavily armored to protect it from antiaircraft fire. The A-10 carries several kinds of bombs and missiles. It also has a powerful machine gun mounted in its nose that can shred a heavily armored tank in seconds.

The AFA program lasts four years. Graduates become air force officers. They are required to serve at least five years in the air force. Pilots have to serve for at least 10 years. Many AFA graduates spend their entire careers in the air force.

RESERVE OFFICER TRAINING CORPS

Every year more than 2,000 college students across the United States take part in the Air Force ROTC program. ROTC students are called cadets, just like Air

Air Force Academy cadets have a challenging study schedule. They must work hard to succeed.

Force Academy students. However, ROTC students go to college at more than 100 colleges and universities across the country.

Most cadets participate in ROTC for four years. During the first two years of the program, they take regular college classes plus general military classes. Each week they have three hours of military classes. In these classes, they practice drills and teamwork and learn military history. Cadets must have grades of C or higher to stay in the ROTC program.

At the end of their second year, ROTC cadets go to an air force base for a four-week training camp. During this difficult camp, the cadets practice military skills. Once they have finished training camp, cadets can apply to continue the ROTC program.

Cadets are allowed to continue into the third year of the ROTC program based on their grades, a physical exam, and their commander's recommendation.

Before piloting aircraft, cadets practice their skills using high-tech flight simulators.

If they are accepted into this selective program, cadets begin their third year of college as members of the U.S. Air Force Reserve. They then receive a scholarship to cover tuition, the year's textbooks, and lab fees. These students also receive $250 to $400 spending money each month they are in school.

During these last two years, cadets learn about being an air force officer. They take classes to prepare them for being a leader. When they graduate from college, they become officers. They are required to serve in the air force for at least four years after graduation.

Air Force Academy cadets celebrate graduation. The Thunderbirds, the air force's performance flight team, roars overhead.

THE THUNDERBIRDS

The Thunderbirds are the U.S. Air Force's air demonstration squadron. The team performs its spectacular, death-defying maneuvers at air shows around the world. Air force leaders created the Thunderbirds in the early 1950s as a way to display the skills of air force pilots and to demonstrate the abilities of the air force's top fighter planes.

The Thunderbird demonstration team has six F-16 Fighting Falcons. Only the air force's top pilots are selected for the team. Selection to the Thunderbirds is a great honor. Each pilot serves in the squadron for two years. They spend the winter months training for the air show season, which lasts from March to November.

The Thunderbirds perform more than 80 times a year. Each performance lasts about one hour and fifteen minutes. During this time, the Thunderbirds perform about 30 different maneuvers. These include flying in extremely close formation—just a few feet apart—and performing many different kinds of midair rolls and turns. The routine is challenging and dangerous. No Thunderbird has ever crashed while performing.

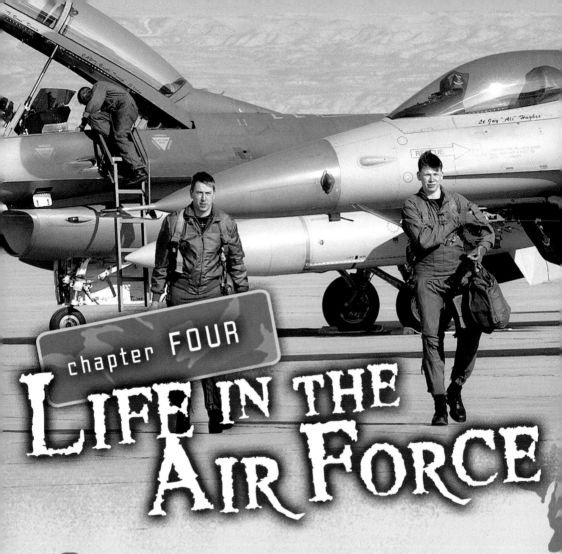

chapter FOUR
LIFE IN THE AIR FORCE

ACTIVE DUTY OFFICERS and airmen
live on air force bases around the world. Bases are
small communities. Each includes an airport. Bases
also have houses, apartments, stores, banks, gas
stations, and other buildings. They usually have their
own post office, library, church, and hospital. Stores
on bases are part of the base exchange (BX). They sell
food and other items. Unmarried airmen and officers
usually live on bases. Married air force members can
live on or off base with their families.

AIR FORCE JOBS

The air force has hundreds of different jobs. More than 10,000 air force officers are pilots. They fly large and small airplanes, as well as helicopters. Even after they become officers, pilots spend most of their time training to fly planes.

Pilots who fly combat planes receive many hours of hard training. They must train with their planes' weapons systems. They must be skilled at reading maps and studying the landscape below them. Combat pilots learn to locate small targets on the ground from high above. Dropping a bomb or firing a missile at the wrong spot could lead to accidental deaths. Combat

Piloting modern fighter aircraft is one of the most exciting and challenging jobs in the world.

pilots must also know what to do if they are shot down over enemy territory.

Pilots are often sent to special training bases. One of these training bases is Nellis Air Force Base in Nevada. At Nellis, pilots practice flying fighter planes. They pretend they are in real battles with the enemy and use real tactics.

Not all air force pilots fly in combat. Some fly cargo planes that carry people and equipment. Others fly helicopters that perform many duties, such as transporting troops and equipment and rescuing downed pilots.

Some officers collect intelligence. This means they gather information about enemies and other countries' air forces. They try to learn what kinds of weapons other countries have. During war, intelligence officers try to

FLIGHT SIMULATORS

Flight simulators are machines that give pilots a chance to test and improve their skills without the danger of flying. Simulators are like super high-tech video games. A pilot steps into a "virtual cockpit." There the pilot is surrounded by computer screens that show nearly everything that can really be seen when flying— including friendly planes, enemy planes, and the ground.

Pilots in flight simulators can also communicate with the rest of their team, just as they would in a real flight. Only instead of being on the same plane, the team members may be thousands of miles away in a different flight simulator.

break enemy codes to find out what the enemy is doing and planning.

Controllers perform another air force job. Controllers use radar and computers to track aircraft in the sky and guide pilots in flight. Some controllers work at bases on the ground. Others work in aircraft that fly high above battlefields. Some controllers are called combat controllers. These people sneak into enemy territory to help U.S. planes find targets. They use equipment to pinpoint targets for aircraft in the sky.

This airman works as an air traffic controller. She uses radar equipment to keep track of aircraft in the air.

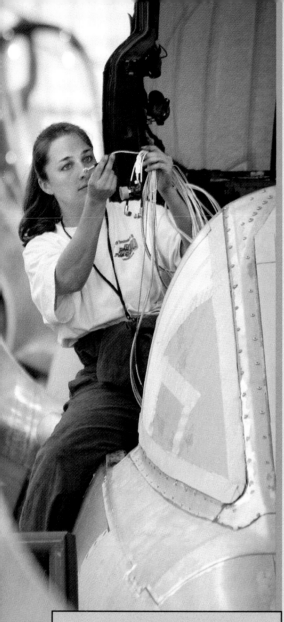

Then the aircraft come in and destroy the targets.

Many airmen are mechanics. Mechanics repair aircraft and other equipment. They test airplanes before and after flights. This is to make sure the planes are safe for flying.

Space exploration is a big part of the air force. Many astronauts are air force members. The air force also helps design, test, and repair spacecraft.

Air force members have lots of other jobs. Many of these have nothing to do with airplanes, flying, or fighting. The air force needs many different kinds of people doing many different jobs to keep it going. Other jobs include work as doctors, nurses, lawyers, bus drivers, cooks, recruiters, police, and lots of other duties. No matter what their job, air force members share and work

Air force mechanics work on some of the most sophisticated machines in the world.

An air force lawyer *(right)* researches a legal case.
Air Force lawyers work on legal cases involving
the air force and its personnel.

toward the same goal. They are all ready to defend the
United States.

AIR FORCE RESERVE

Some officers and airmen join the air force part-time.
They serve as part of the U.S. Air Force Reserve. Reserve
members, called reservists, train for one weekend each month. They also go to a full-time training camp for one or two weeks each year. In return, they get a small allowance from the air force.

Some officers and airmen join the air force part-time. These people serve as part of the U.S. Air Force Reserve. Reserve members train for one weekend each month.

INSIGNIA

LIKE ALL OF THE U.S. ARMED FORCES, the air force is organized according to rank. A person of lower rank is required to follow the orders of someone of higher rank. For example, an airman, the lowest rank, is expected to follow the orders of a master sergeant or a captain. A captain is required to follow the orders of a major or a colonel and so on. The highest air force rank is general of the air force. All air force personnel wear insignia that show their rank. Here are a number of insignia, starting with the lowest rank and moving up to the highest.

ENLISTED PERSONNEL

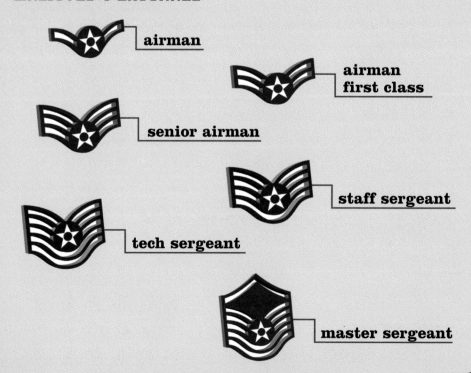

airman

airman
first class

senior airman

staff sergeant

tech sergeant

master sergeant

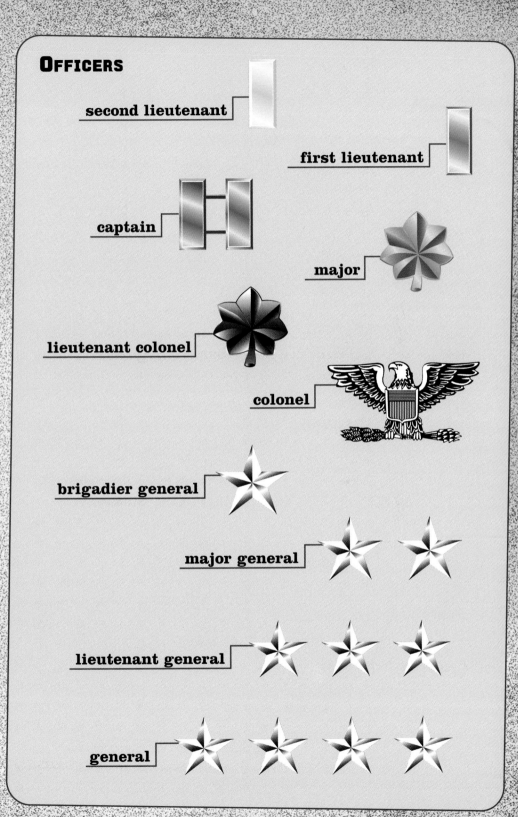

Officers

second lieutenant

first lieutenant

captain

major

lieutenant colonel

colonel

brigadier general

major general

lieutenant general

general

Many reservists are people who have retired from full-time active duty. Others are people who have other jobs. Reservists are ready in case the air force needs more people. For example, if a war starts, the air force may place reserve members on full-time active duty.

NEW EQUIPMENT

Air force members are always training and developing new ways to defend the country. In the 2000s, many countries continue to develop ICBMs. U.S. leaders fear such missiles could be used against the United States. The air force is working to develop weapons that can destroy these missiles in case they are launched. This weapons system is called the Airborne Laser System. Air force planes will carry these weapons. They will be able to shoot

AIR FORCE AIRCRAFT DESIGNATIONS

Each model of aircraft in air force service has a designating letter and number. The letter describes the aircraft's role. The number stands for the model of aircraft.

A = attack plane. These include the A-10 Thunderbolt, which attacks ground targets to help troops on the ground.

B = bomber. This class includes large, long-range bombers, such as the B-52 and B-2.

C = cargo. Cargo planes such as the C-130 and C-17 transport people and equipment.

F = fighter. The F-15 Eagle, the F-16 Fighting Falcon, and other fighters are designed to fight enemy aircraft in the air. They can also attack ground targets.

H = helicopter. The air force uses many different kinds of helicopters for combat and for other duties.

T = trainer. Pilots develop their flight skills in training aircraft such as the T-88.

Some U.S. aircraft have many roles and many designations, such as the F/A-18 and the AC-130.

This Boeing 747 jumbo jet will be adapted to hold the Airborne Laser System. The powerful missile-destroying laser will be mounted in the jet's nose.

lasers (powerful beams of light) at enemy missiles to destroy them.

The air force is also working with companies to develop new and better airplanes to help defend the country. The newest fighter is another stealth aircraft, the F-22 Raptor. The Raptor's design makes it hard to detect with radar. Raptors are extremely fast. They also have new computers that help pilots locate enemy targets.

Another new aircraft is the F-35 Joint Strike Fighter (JSF). Like the F-22, the JSF is fast and stealthy. It will also be used by the British Royal Air Force. Air force leaders and pilots are working with aircraft makers to develop the F-35 for the future.

RAPID RESPONSE

More and more, a quick response is important for
saving lives and avoiding wars. When trouble starts in
one part of the world, the U.S. military needs to act
quickly. Quick responses can sometimes end fighting
before it becomes more serious.

Members of a rapid response squadron load equipment and
material into a C-5 Galaxy for use in Afghanistan.

The air force is ready to fly to any part of the world
on short notice. Special quick-response wings are
located at Langley Air Force Base in Virginia. These
wings have fighter, bomber, and transport planes that
are ready to fly anyplace, anytime.

SPACE EXPLORATION

Space exploration is a major part of the air force's work. The air force helps develop many space projects for the United States. Air force pilots have piloted space shuttles. They have also flown to the moon.

The air force continues to work with U.S. companies to develop satellites. Newer satellites are very powerful. Spy satellites circle hundreds or even thousands of miles above the earth. They can take very clear photographs of the ground below. The satellites are used for reconnaissance. They can also detect if a country has launched missiles or made other hostile acts. During peacetime, spy satellites are used to help U.S. leaders know if other countries might be a threat.

Astronaut Bruce McCandless II on a space walk during a flight of the space shuttle

MISSIONS

The U.S. Air Force performs two kinds of missions: strategic and tactical. Strategic missions try to cut an enemy's ability to wage war and discourage its people. These missions include dropping bombs or shooting missiles at an enemy's cities, roads, and communications systems. Tactical missions provide direct support for ground fighting. For instance, shooting at enemy troops is a tactical mission.

F-16 Fighting Falcons soar high in the sky above the United States. Air force personnel are always on duty, protecting the nation's skies.

THE FUTURE

In 2007 the U.S. Air Force will turn 60 years old. In less than 60 years, this branch of the armed forces has had many great accomplishments. Air force airmen and officers have helped the United States to win several wars. They have also helped to prevent many more wars around the world.

In the future, the men and women of the U.S. Air Force will continue to defend the United States. They will also continue to help out wherever they are needed around the world.

AIR FORCE ONE

One of the U.S. Air Force's most important jobs is flying the president of the United States across the country and around the world. The air force is responsible for flying and maintaining the two identical presidential planes. When the president is aboard one of these planes, the aircraft is known as Air Force One *(above)*.

The presidential aircraft are Boeing 747 jumbo jets. They have been adapted in many ways for the president. While most 747s have dozens of rows of aisles and seats, the Air Force One aircraft have offices, sleeping areas, a conference/dining room, and two kitchens (known as galleys). The aircraft also have high-tech communications systems and a medical area where doctors can treat medical emergencies.

Unlike most other 747s, the presidential aircraft have also been adapted for midair refueling. This allows the president and crew to stay airborne for days, if necessary. This also allows the president to stay high in the sky, away from crisis situations, such as a nuclear attack.

The presidential aircraft have a crew of 26 people, including their air force pilots. Each plane can hold a total of 102 people, allowing the president to invite along friends, fellow leaders, assistants, and newspaper and television reporters on presidential trips.

STRUCTURE

THE AIR FORCE IS ORGANIZED around pilots and their planes. Each plane and pilot belongs to a unit called a flight. All air force members who support those planes also belong to the flight. Several flights make up a squadron. Four or more squadrons make up a larger unit called a wing. A wing may have a few hundred planes.

Several wings make up a command, the largest unit in the air force. All together, the U.S. Air Force is made up of nine commands. A four-star general heads each major command.

The Department of the Air Force is in charge of all of the commands. Two people are in charge at the Department of the Air Force. One is a military commander, called the chief of staff. The other is a civilian, or nonmilitary, commander called the secretary of the air force. Both of these commanders report to the U.S. secretary of defense, who reports to the president of the United States.

PRESIDENT OF THE UNITED STATES

SECRETARY OF DEFENSE

SECRETARY OF THE AIR FORCE

AIR FORCE CHIEF OF STAFF

COMMAND

WING

SQUADRON

FLIGHT

TIMELINE

1903 The Wright brothers complete the world's first airplane flight.

1907 The U.S. Army Air Service is formed.

1917 The United States enters World War I. The first U.S. planes are flown in combat.

1941 The United States enters World War II. The U.S. Army Air Forces are formed.

1945 World War II ends.

1947 The air force becomes a separate branch of the military. Air force pilot Chuck Yeager becomes the first person to fly faster than the speed of sound.

1950 The Korean War begins. The U.S. Air Force uses a powerful new plane called the F-86 Sabre.

1960s The United States becomes involved in the Vietnam War. USAF aircraft and personnel attack North Vietnamese targets.

1969 USAF lieutenant colonel Edwin "Buzz" Aldrin becomes the second person to walk on the moon.

1991 On January 17, coalition forces, led by the United States, remove Iraqi forces from Kuwait. USAF aircraft and personnel help coalition forces.

1992 The United States sends troops to Somalia. USAF forces support them.

1993 Women are allowed to become air force pilots.

1995 The United States and other countries step into the war in Bosnia. Marcelite (Marcie) Harris is awarded the rank of major general. She is the first African American woman to achieve this rank.

1999 The United States and other countries join the war in Serbia.

2001 Terrorists attack New York and Washington, D.C., on September 11. U.S. forces invade Afghanistan on October 7. USAF pilots fly many missions in support of U.S. troops.

2003 Coalition forces invade Iraq on March 19. USAF pilots bomb Baghdad and provide CAS for coalition troops.

GLOSSARY

biplanes: small, slow airplanes with two sets of wings

boot camp: basic military training; the first training for enlisted members

cadet: a student at the Air Force Academy or in the Reserve Officer Training Corps

civilian: any nonmilitary person

combat: active fighting; battle

controller: a person who guides flights using radar and computers

dogfight: a battle where aircraft shoot at each other, trying to knock one another out of the sky

enlist: to join one of the branches of the armed services. Enlisted members of the air force are called airmen.

mechanic: an airman who repairs airplanes and other equipment

radar: machinery that uses radio waves to locate objects, usually in the air

reconnaissance: scouting, or gathering information

recruit: airman in training

satellite: a spacecraft that circles the earth to gather information and send signals

stealth planes: airplanes that are hard for enemy radar to detect

FAMOUS PEOPLE

Lieutenant Colonel Edwin "Buzz" Aldrin (born 1930) Born in New Jersey, Aldrin served as a combat pilot during the Korean War. He later became an astronaut. On July 20, 1969, he landed on the moon with Neil Armstrong. Aldrin became the second person to walk on the moon.

General Henry "Hap" Arnold (1886–1950) Born in Pennsylvania, Arnold learned to fly from the Wright brothers, flight pioneers. He joined the U.S. Army in 1907. Arnold served as commanding general of the U.S. Army Air Forces during World War II. He helped create the air force as a separate military branch in 1947. General Arnold later became the air force's first and only five-star general.

Colonel Jacqueline "Jackie" Cochran (1908–1980) Born in Florida, Cochran was a famous female pilot in the 1920s and 1930s. She later joined the air force and created the Women's Airforce Service Pilots (WASPs) during World War II. In 1953 she became the first woman to fly faster than the speed of sound.

General Benjamin O. Davis Jr. (1912–2002) Born in Washington, D.C., Davis commanded the Tuskegee Airmen during World War II. The Tuskegee Airmen were the first group of African American AAF fighter pilots.

General Daniel "Chappie" James Jr. (1920–1978) Born in Florida, James was a fighter pilot in World War II, the Korean War, and the Vietnam War. He later became the air force's first African-American four-star general.

Major Alton Glenn Miller (1904–1944) Born in Iowa, Glenn Miller was one of the most popular musicians in the United States during the 1930s and 1940s. In 1942 Miller joined the army air force. He formed the Major Glenn Miller Army Air Force Band, and his group traveled around the world entertaining troops during the war. In 1944 he boarded a plane in England to fly to France. But the plane disappeared, and Miller was never found.

Brigadier General Charles "Chuck" Yeager (born 1923) Born in West Virginia, Yeager was a fighter pilot in Europe during World War II. After the war, he became a test pilot for the air force. In October 1947, he became the first person to fly faster than the speed of sound.

BIBLIOGRAPHY

Air Force Link. The Official Site of the U.S. Air Force. 2004. <http://www.af.mil> (February 2004).

Boyne, Walter J. *Beyond the Blue: A History of the U.S. Air Force, 1947–1997.* New York: St. Martin's Press, 1997.

Burgan, Michael. *The World's Fastest Military Airplanes.* Mankato, MN: Capstone Books, 2001.

Green, Michael. *The United States Air Force.* Mankato, MN: Capstone High/Low Books, 1998.

Kennedy, Robert C. *Life as an Air Force Fighter Pilot.* New York: Children's Press, 2000.

Langley, Wanda. *The Air Force in Action.* Berkeley Heights, NJ: Enslow Publishers, 2001.

Lloyd, Alwyn T. *A Cold War Legacy: A Tribute to Strategic Air Command, 1946–1992.* Missoula, MT: Pictorial Histories Publishing Company, Inc., 1999.

Sievert, Terri. *The U.S. Air Force at War.* Mankato, MN: Capstone High-Interest Books, 2002.

FURTHER READING

Cornish, Geoff. *Battlefield Support.* Minneapolis, MN: Lerner Publications Company, 2003.

Dartford, Mark. *Bombers.* Minneapolis, MN: Lerner Publications Company, 2003.

____. *Fighter Planes.* Minneapolis, MN: Lerner Publications Company, 2003.

____. *Helicopters.* Minneapolis, MN: Lerner Publications Company, 2003.

____. *Missiles and Rockets.* Minneapolis, MN: Lerner Publications Company, 2003.

Fredriksen, John C. *Warbirds: An Illustrated Guide to U.S. Military Aircraft, 1915-2000.* Santa Barbara, CA: ABC-Clio, Inc., 1999.

Gunston, Bill. *The Illustrated Directory of Fighting Aircraft of World War II.* Osceola, WI: MBI Publishing Company, 2001.

Lake, John. *The Great Book of Bombers: The World's Most Important Bombers from World War I to the Present Day.* St. Paul, MN: MBI Publishing Company, 2002.

Sweetman, Bill. *F-22 Raptor.* Osceola, WI: Motorbooks International, 1998.

WEBSITES

Airborne Laser System
<http://www.boeing.com/defense-space/military/abl/flash.html>
Follow the development of the Airborne Laser System at the
official site of its developer, Boeing.

Air Force Link Junior
<http://www.af.mil/aflinkjr>
This USAF site provides fun and games for kids, while
teaching about the air force's history and role.

Air Force One
<http://www.boeing.com/defense-space/military/af1/flash.html>
Learn more about the presidential aircraft from Air Force
One's official website.

Air Force Recruitment Services
<http://www.airforce.com>
Learn more about careers and how to enlist in the USAF from
its official recruiting website.

U.S. Air Force Academy
<http://www.usafa.af.mil>
Learn more about the Air Force Academy, from the Academy's
official website.

U.S. Air Force Museum
<http://www.wpafb.af.mil/museum>
Visit the USAF Museum's online exhibits at this website.

The United States Air Force Thunderbirds
<http://www.airforce.com/thunderbirds/>
The official website of the Thunderbirds has information on
Thunderbird team members, the squadron's performance
schedule, a history of the team, and an interactive Web page
with information about the Thunderbirds' aircraft, the F-16
Fighting Falcon.

Index

ABOUT THE AUTHOR

Sandy Donovan has written numerous books for young readers on topics including history, civics, and biology. Donovan has also worked as a newspaper reporter and a magazine editor. She holds a bachelor's degree in journalism and a master's degree in public policy. Her titles include *U.S. Naval Special Warfare Forces*, *The Channel Tunnel*, *Making Laws: A Look at How a Bill Becomes a Law*, *Protecting America: A Look at the People Who Keep Our Country Safe*, and *Running for Office: A Look at Political Campaigns*. Donovan lives in Minneapolis with her husband and two sons.

PHOTO ACKNOWLEDGMENTS

The images in this book are used with the permission of: Defense Visual Information Center (DVIC), pp. 4, 11, 13, 14, 15, 16, 18, 24, 25, 26, 28 (bottom), 29 (top), 32, 34 (both), 36 (all) 37 (top and middle), 38, 39, 42, 43, 44, 47, 52, 53; © Hulton|Archive by Getty Images, p. 5; © Bettmann/CORBIS, pp. 6, 8, 10; National Archives, p. 7; courtesy of the U.S. Air Force, pp. 12, 19, 20, 21, 23, 33, 37 (bottom), 40, 41, 45, 46, 48 (all), 49 (all), 55; © Photri, Inc., p. 28 (top); © Najlah Feanny/CORBIS, p. 29 (bottom); © CORBIS, p. 31; © The Boeing Corporation, p. 51; © George Hall/CORBIS, p. 54.

Cover: courtesy of the U.S. Air Force.